Understanding Narcissism:
Healing and finding yourself again

OrangeBooks Publication

1st Floor, Rajhans Arcade, Mall Road, Kohka, Bhilai, Chhattisgarh 490020

Website:**www.orangebooks.in**

© Copyright, 2024, Author

All rights reserved. No part of this book may be reproduced, stored in a retrieval system, or transmitted, in any form by any means, electronic, mechanical, magnetic, optical, chemical, manual, photocopying, recording or otherwise, without the prior written consent of its writer.

First Edition, 2024
ISBN: 978-93-5621-454-5

UNDERSTANDING NARCISSISM

Healing and finding yourself again

RUNA GANGULY

OrangeBooks Publication
www.orangebooks.in

Introduction

There are various mental illnesses that we know of. The likes of ADHD, Depression, Bipolar Disorder, Anxiety Disorder, etc. affect the patients more on a personal level. Not only are these identifiable but the behavior of the patient can be rectified if the right kind of help is received. Very rarely do the people around them bear the scars of their behavioral traits. Even if they do, it is not very difficult to overcome and deal with them.

On the other spectrum, Narcissism is a diagnosed mental or personality disorder that leaves the people living with them in a traumatic situation and robs them of their individuality. Very rarely will the survivor know that they are suffering at the hands of a narcissist. A narcissist carries a lot of psychological damage, mostly from their childhood. Even if a few recognize that they indeed carry narcissistic symptoms and need treatment, acknowledging the same and getting proper help is something that a narcissist will very rarely do.

This book does not aim to rebuke or demean narcissism as a mental disorder. I believe by acknowledging and seeking proper professional help, any mental health survivor can turn their lives around.

I have been raised in a family with narcissistic parents and have been married to one for over a decade. I am still in touch with my parents and ex, as we share a child together. It took me a while to understand what narcissism is, and on my journey to self-realization and healing, I have learnt to distance myself from toxic attachments as far as possible. This book is an account on my healing journey without making any personal references.

Hoping this provides you with the clarity you need and also a way forward. My next publication will be focused on self-acceptance, identifying wrong attachment styles to people and forging and maintaining healthier relationships.

Table of Content

Introduction..v

Chapter One 1
Narcissists: How to Identify Them?............................2

Chapter Two 8
Quitting A Narcissistic Bond 9

Chapter Three 17
Healing After Separation from A Narcissist..................18

Chapter ONE

Narcissists: How to Identify Them?

Now that we hear and read about *"narcissistic"* people, we understand that knowingly or unknowingly, we all have come across or could have even lived with narcissistic individuals at some point in our lives.

So, how do we identify and avoid narcissistic people?

Narcissistic individuals are highly capable of disguising themselves to make you believe who they are not. It is only when they are fully confident that you trust them no matter what that is the time they slowly reveal themselves. Here are some prominent traits a narcissistic person would exhibit:

1. Victim Mentality:

A narcissist will always insist on being the victim. They will find a way to blame the survivor by speaking of their ways and means, how badly their life is affected because of the survivor, certain situations, etc. Taking ownership of their actions and wrong decisions is something that they would never do. This trait becomes more prominent when the survivor finally decides to separate from the narcissist.

2. Making you question yourself:

"Even if you start your own business, you would fail."

"I suggest you really think this through again."

Sounds familiar? A narcissist will time and again make you question yourself whenever you decide anything on your own without including them in the process. This trait is very dominant when you try to become independent or plan to make a life-changing decision. They would even know that you are fully capable of achieving what you set your eyes on, but then they fear losing control over your mind.

3. Attacking your social life:

One of the prominent traits of narcissists is that they will always be uncomfortable with your social life. This may include your own family, friends, colleagues, etc. They constantly fear losing control over your mind if someone in your social circuit tries to influence your thoughts in a way that does not benefit them.

To attain this goal, they will always keep checking who you meet on a daily basis, what your colleagues say, the family details of your friends, etc. They will try to associate or attribute any random dispute or disagreement to the quality of your social circle. Cutting you free from your social circle would mean that you would only look up to them for answers or any kind of support, especially emotional.

4. Ensuring dependency, especially financial:

One of the biggest achievements of a narcissist would be to make you feel emotionally and financially dependent on you. In a marriage (irrespective of gender), they may come up with sugar-coated lines like:

"Why don't you let me take care of the finances, you can tend to the kids. They are growing up and need your attention."

"My money is yours; you don't need to worry about finances."

They know by clipping your wings and making you financially dependent on them, they can eventually block you from leaving them in the future.

5. Ignoring your emotional needs:

A narcissist would say and do all the right things at the beginning until they win your trust completely. In a relationship, they would leave work early for you, show up on time, drop you home safely and all. They make you believe how mature and dependent they are.

It is only after you are in a committed relationship with them; you would notice this sense of trying to control you because of the fear of losing you someday. They would make you wait, ignore your feelings and needs and make you yearn and chase them just to reaffirm themselves that you still and will always need them.

In a work set, you can see a narcissistic boss or a co-worker turning into a complete opposite version of what they showed during the interviews or initially orienting you into the company.

6. Judgemental, insecure and jealous:

A narcissist would never admit it, but they are never secure with what they are or have. They would be always envy with what someone else has. It is as if nothing and nobody is good enough for them. They may come across as confident socially, but deep down, they are very insecure about losing out to people or losing their friends or partner to someone better.

Judging people based on their social life, their social media posts and how they dress or basically look on the outside is very common for a narcissistic person, and again, they know how to mask this trait and would not admit to this either.

7. Friends and family are always above you:

This one is for survivors of narcissistic life partners. You will have to compete with their friends and family to get the validity of your narcissistic partner. They would always value the opinions of their friends and family above yours.

Very often, you will find yourself in a situation where, say, if you narrate an issue at work where you have been bullied or played by one of your colleagues, more often than not, your narcissistic partner would blame you for the issue and show the errors in your ways. Now, if their own friends or family members are ever in a similar situation, they will be all out in support of them and narrate their agony to you, painting them as the victim.

They are closely knit to people who have been in their lives for longer than how you have been and value them, as they do not shun them away or see anything wrong in them. If you speak anything against them, they would freak out and even start an argument, blaming you for dragging them away from their friends or family.

8. Closeness to a mother or a narcissistic parent:

A narcissistic spouse would be extremely attached to their narcissistic parent; in most cases, it will be their mother. Your narcissistic partner would always turn to their mother whenever they need someone to stroke their ego and validate their beliefs. Just like friends and family members, no words would be tolerated against their mother. Their unhealthy competitive nature and *"I am always right"* feelings were developed earlier on in life, mostly shaped by a narcissistic parent.

9. Never feels loved or appreciated by you:

A narcissistic spouse will never admit what and how much you do for them or for the family. They will always remind you of how their friends and family praise them and value them, and you don't.

Even if they praise or appreciate you for a particular skill or what you did for them, they would always expect praise back for something. If you fail to do so, they will keep that in mind and will bring it up sometime in the future. They always feel they have or already had offered enough of their time, attention or love to you, and you do not reciprocate the same way.

10. Feeling entitled:

A narcissist would always want you to be isolated and feel powerless. They mostly treat the survivor like their possession and not as an individual. It is as if you exist to support them or as an accessory in their lives.

You will have to explain your whereabouts whenever you are out without them; you have to provide details of your friends, colleagues, etc. Now, try doing the same with them, and the reply would be…

"Why are you being such a control freak?"

"You are so frustrated; you need to get a life!"

"You don't trust me?"

Having control over your whereabouts and even what you do or think on a daily basis makes them feel in control of their lives.

11. Manipulating therapist:

If you are in a bad marriage with a narcissist, getting them to see a counsellor will be a daunting task. They would hate you stating your opinions to a third person and being judged and evaluated. They would, at the most, agree to go to a one-to-one counselling session, not a joint one.

The reason is that it is always easier for them to manipulate the counsellor and come on top of the discussion looking like the one suffering and miserable. Yes! A narcissist is quite capable of fooling a trained therapist into believing their side of the story.

Even if you do convince them to see a marriage counsellor for joint therapy, more often than not, you would end up being judged as the cause of the unhappy relationship. They would prepare themselves in advance on how to counter all your points and come out as the one who is suffering. The counselling would only leave you confused and, at times, doubt yourself if what they are stating is true.

12. They have to win and are ALWAYS right:

Not only will they never agree on the errors in their ways, but they will refuse to even listen and accept anything wrong about their loyal family members and friends. They have to be at the top of all the discussions and come out a winner in all the arguments.

They know this trait in themselves and hence often mention to you, *"relationships are not about competing"*, making you look like the one in competition with them always!

Thus, if you are in a long-term relationship with a narcissist, there will be a point in life where, for the sake of your own peace, you would just avoid arguments. You will avoid even small talk during meals or when outdoors because you never know their reactions to specific situations and topics.

Concluding Words:

To conclude this chapter, it is imperative for you to understand that not all narcissistic individuals would display all the traits mentioned here. Remember, a narcissistic spouse, boss, or friend has a specific mould in their mind for you, and it is about how they see you fitting in that mould to be of use to them. The moment you start to display signs of protest and disagreement, they feel the need to control you before they lose you completely.

In the next chapter, let us look at what happens when you finally realise that you have been living with a Narcissistic person and decide to call it quits.

Chapter TWO

Quitting A Narcissistic Bond

It is imperative here to know that it is never easy for anyone to quit a narcissist, given the trauma bonding they have with the narcissist. *Trauma bonding,* in simple terms, means an unhealthy attachment.

Most of the illustrations mentioned below will be with regard to personal relationships, but it's important to understand that the narcissistic behaviour pattern in any relationship will be almost similar. It is, in fact, more difficult to break free from a family attachment as we are emotionally bonded to that person.

Let us now explore:

A. How a narcissist keeps a victim in a trauma bond?

B. Why is it difficult to quit the trauma bond with a narcissist?

C. The narcissist's reaction when the victim finally calls it quits.

A. In order to understand the entire cycle of identifying narcissistic traits to healing yourself, let us try to know how a narcissist keeps the victim trauma bound:

It is of great interest to the narcissist to keep the victim feeling low and inadequate. They demand blind trust and loyalty. Eventually, the victim becomes guarded and avoids reacting so as not to trigger the narcissist.

They would always want the victim to think that they are the problem. The narcissist will always be unwilling to examine themselves and work on their issues. So, how and what drives them to have this kind of bonding with the victim?

1. Trauma bonding allows them to manage their pain:

The only way they see a victory or a solution to manage their inner struggles is to create more pain in someone else's life. When someone feels inadequate, they feel validated. It is a way to take the focus off or gain a diversion from their own internal struggles.

2. It makes them feel on top all the time:

By maintaining a trauma bond, they compensate for fear of powerlessness. Relationship in their mind is built on the equation of 'dominance and submission'. Getting them to keep the victim in the submission mode helps them to build their pitiable ego.

Most narcissists have been subjected to a lot of judgement and rejection in the past. So, seeing the victim suffer emotionally gives them a power rush and a feeling that they are much better than them.

3. Denying their own insecurities and fears:

As mentioned earlier, most narcissists have unaddressed childhood traumas. If they have been neglected or ill-treated by their parents or one of their parents, they try to fill that void by seeking that love and compassion from others as they grow up.

When they find an empath or someone giving and caring, they are sure to attach themselves to that person. In reality, it is not the empath they are in love with; it is their energy or vibes which they adore. This leads us to our next point.

4. Bread crumbing:

We must have all heard about this. A narcissist uses this technique of showing off or giving away just enough to make it look as if they are into the victim or serious about them. In reality, it only means they look at the victim as an asset who can be pulled off the shelf, used when needed and kept them back there when they are done.

They will especially show off morsels of love and compassion when they know they have been over the edge or when the victim shows signs of understanding their behaviour and resents them.

They like to keep their options open and will ghost the victims mostly after a favourable time with them. They would, however, not close a chapter with anyone and keep the doors open so that they can resurface in their lives as and when they need you.

In a work-related scenario, it could be a potential partner ghosting you after you thought you could be a great team together. In a personal relationship, the person may choose to disappear after a sexual encounter.

Bread crumbing can also be done by narcissists who are in a long and committed relationship. They will show off love and generosity as and when they need to, especially in social settings or in a family gathering. Otherwise, you will find them in total ignorance of your emotional needs. At some point in a day, they can be a loving partner and then, within a few minutes, turn cold and ignorant, making you wonder if you even exist for them.

5. Future faking:

Many of the victims are sucked into the narcissist's strategy of future faking and making them believe that they are aware of their issues and would work towards them. They would use phrases like:

- 'You know I just started this new business and it's been tough for me. I didn't mean to...'
- 'The holiday season is always tough for us. Let us give this some more time and I am sure we can work through this'... and so on.

They keep the victim stuck by giving them false hope to fall back on and making them forget about their concerns for the time being.

All these strategies mentioned above make it easy for a narcissist to keep the victim trauma-bound. It is thus important to understand that is normal for the victim to procrastinate leaving the narcissist while in a trauma bond.

B. Now, is it only the trauma bond, or does a victim have other reasons for not quitting on the narcissist?

A victim may have one or all the following reasons for being unable to quit a narcissist:

➤ Bad or traumatic childhood:

One reason why a victim can feel trapped and difficult to break free from a narcissist trauma bond is because they unknowingly grew up with parents, siblings or friends who were narcissistic. So, for many, it becomes difficult and almost impossible to identify with normal behaviour. Even if the narcissistic individual displays certain red flags at the beginning, they are too unaware to see them.

➤ Develop a sense of false optimism:

Trauma bonding gives the victim a false sense of security. They start to overlook certain controlling behaviour of the narcissist by telling themselves, 'We can work through it'. They start future faking and moving their own goal post of quitting them.

➤ Fear of another breakup:

If the victim had other bad relationships in the past, they may fear being lonely once again after walking away from the narcissist. So, they 'hang in there', hoping for things to change someday.

➤ Financial or family concern:

Quitting on a narcissistic partner, especially when a victim is not financially independent or has dependent children, appears seemingly impossible.

➤ Enablers:

There are certain 'enablers', who would not have a clue of the victim's day to day mental turmoil, but will appear to be an empath and downplay the entire concern and make them second guess themselves. They may mention:

- 'Oh, come on, these things are common in every relationship,'

- 'You are taking this too far,' or
- 'You need to give them another chance by going through a therapy session together,'...and so on.

Deciding to quit on a narcissistic becomes difficult if one is constantly made to guess themselves second. Enablers could be parents, friends, colleagues, etc.

➤ Comfort zone:

Many victims fear change, as it is better to be with a 'known devil'. So, they keep hoping and praying that this phase in their lives changes someday. Leaving a narcissist behind means a huge change in their lives, which they are not ready to make.

C. Quitting stage:

Now that after all the procrastination, when you finally decide to quit the narcissist, you know it is not going to be easy and that they are not going to be very receptive of your decision.

To be well prepared in the process, let us now try and figure out what goes inside the mind of a narcissist when you call it quits.

Remember, the main GOAL of the narcissist is to wear you down. If you are repeatedly subjected to most of the behaviour tactics mentioned above, it causes you:

- Emotional fatigue
- Second-guessing yourself
- Feeling inadequate and
- Feeling of resentment

Now, when you try to break free from them, they see it as an audacious move on your side. It hits them off guard, striking the very core of their being. It unleashes an emotional storm, tearing them apart from within.

Many narcissists downplay its significance by telling themselves that 'it is just another breakup' or a temporary setback. Denial can give them some initial relief, and they can pretend and try hard to look happy, especially socially or at work.

Once it sinks in that you are really gone, they start the blame game. Anger consumes them, as they find every reason to blame you for their mental turmoil. They would assert that they have been used by you and that you never really loved or cared for them. Once they know you are not returning, they question as to how you could be so heartless to abandon them in such a manner.

Few may even get into a new relationship with unprocessed emotion and resentment towards you, only burdening their new person with their trauma and anger. It is important for them to latch on to someone and feed off their energy as they feel empty from within.

They may also indulge in vindictive and obsessive behaviour to hit back at you and to shame you. While they do so, they are also finding your replacement to forge new connections. They will avoid taking any accountability and rationalise their actions, thus victimising themselves.

Many may openly show off socially that they have moved on since you left. But the truth is that they also secretly hope that you will come crawling back someday.

It just showcases their fear of life and their constant urge to be in control. They will also try to connect with common friends and family members to 'sell' their side of the story, which makes them look like the victim. By making you the offender, they will try to cut you off from the social support group that you once thought you always had.

If you share children with a narcissistic partner, be prepared for them to use the children as pawns, manipulating them emotionally to inflict harm upon you and to cause you guilt and shame.

Once you decide to quit, and even after quitting, you need to, for quite sometime, remind yourself *to stay strong* so as not to get sucked back into the same toxic cycle over and over again. Remember, you chose to be a Survivor and a Fighter, instead of being a victim.

Understanding Co-dependency:

Quitting narcissistic family member /parent(s):

Most of us find it extremely difficult to quit on and distance ourselves from narcissistic parent(s). The toxic loyalty is deep rooted and being the only person in a toxic family who is aware of being abused, leads us to loneliness. Hence, it is easier to ignore the signs and pretend that things are fine because our family is all we have when we have no one to turn to. This is *'co-dependency'*.

We may easily talk to a therapists or good friends about a toxic boss or a narcissistic partner, but it is extremely 'shameful' to admit and open up about a toxic family and especially, parents. Many of us not only try to convince ourselves, but also have to also convince a sibling or a family member to adjust, let go or grow-up from the abuse faced at the hands of toxic parents.

We might tell ourselves or others:

- 'Yeah, but... she's our mom. You know what a hard life she had!' or
- 'I have got over it, shouldn't you have by now'?

We are not only protective of our toxic family or parents, but also get triggered when a significant other, for example our partner, realises this and makes a mention of the same. We live and convince ourselves of a distorted reality rooted in toxic loyalty.

We not only disregard someone's opinion but also fail to embrace the truth, which is needed to walk out on toxic relationships. We need to remind ourselves that we can only help a toxic person to realise the truth, but they have their own path in this lifetime.

As mentioned above, it is not possible to completely cut yourself from a toxic person when we share responsibilities, but we can always maintain healthy boundaries so as to concentrate on our own healing journey.

Conclusion:

This chapter dealt with how a narcissistic individual keeps the victim trauma-bonded because of their own insecurities and controlling nature. Also, we know that a victim can have their own issues, mostly from the past, that do not allow them to quit on a toxic person very easily.

In the next chapter pertaining to healing, we will take this forward and understand the concept of *co-dependency* in detail while addressing the various issues we develop in our childhood that lead us to make unhealthy choices in relationships.

Chapter THREE

Healing After Separation from A Narcissist

A narcissist makes every possible attempt to prove that their way of behaviour is the 'normal' one. After detaching from a narcissist, you need to first assert yourself by realising who you are supposed to be and not what the narcissist made you believe you were.

Hence, let us understand:

    A. Immediate steps to be taken after detaching from a narcissistic trauma bond

    B. Making the right mindset towards healing.

    C. Cultivating and practicing self-respect.

    D. Inner child healing process

    E. Healing from narcissistic parental abuse.

A. Steps to take after you release yourself from a narcissist:

The first step in quitting a relationship with a narcissist is to remind yourself that you have been in an abusive relationship and you need to free yourself to assert your mental balance and harmony. You have to:

1. Find help:

You need to realise, as mentioned above, that you have been suffering mental abuse for a while or for years, as the case might be. It is important to confide in people who can truly help you without judging your decision.

If you are conscious of the views of friends or family members, you should seek professional help. It is important for someone to reassure you at this time that you have done the right thing and you should stick to your decision. In the absence of proper support, you will feel isolated, doubt yourself and your decision to quit the narcissist and will be easily drawn towards their tactics to suck you back into their life.

2. Avoiding the 'Hoovering cycle': A BIG WARNING!

The term 'hoovering' is normally used when we use a vacuum cleaner to clean the house. In relationships, it indicates a manipulation tactic opted by someone to suck the victim back into a toxic bond.

One big way they do this is by creating a fantasy version for you by 'love bombing'.

They try to show how sorry they are now that you left them and that they really understand how they mistreated you. They really love the chase and this hoovering cycle.

Some or most of us do like people feeling sorry for their wrong actions towards us and easily gravitate towards them if they present themselves the right way. But in this case, it's important to realise that the narcissist is just trying to lure you in like a 'trophy' or a 'toy' that they need to win back. Once they have your trust back, they will bounce back to being themselves.

They will also make sure to remind you of this abandonment incident over and over again to shame you and make you feel guilty. Every trauma-bonded cell in your body can tell you to go back to your 'comfort zone'. But remember, this is the crucial stage in your life. You have a choice to start a new life or get sucked back into the same toxic cycle again.

The need for getting help is, hence, the first step after you detach yourself from a narcissist, as you will be more mentally prepared to deal with the pressures that a narcissist will use to win you back. Detaching the second time from a narcissistic pattern will be even more difficult than the first attempt.

3. 'I miss them' syndrome:

It may sound strange, but most of the survivors actually miss the narcissist after separation. The reason is that living with a narcissist is no less than living with a child; it is a full-time job! You kept thinking all the while, 'How can I please them?', 'How can I win them over?', etc.

They were kind of a 'hobby' in your life, and after separation, you start questioning, 'Do I miss them?', 'Did I make a mistake by leaving them?', and so on. You need to understand that you can miss someone, but it can also be an unhealthy attachment.

4. Physically blocking:

Depending upon the severity of the situation you are in, it is always advisable to maintain a healthy distance from the narcissist after separation. Even if it is not possible to completely avoid the person, find a way and set a boundary so as to have minimal interaction. You need to be alone first and foremost, away from their presence, to even start thinking straight and get on to your feet.

5. Brace yourself for a painful journey before the process of healing starts:

Many suffer for years in a narcissistic attachment for many different reasons, struggling to cope and hoping for a better tomorrow that unfortunately, is never destined to come. The longer you stay in a traumatic situation, the greater the pain of quitting it.

The separation process and the healing journey would not be something that any feeble-minded individual can handle. We all have what it takes to stop and come out of mental abuse, but we fret and procrastinate for several reasons, like the ones mentioned in the earlier chapter.

6. Deserving dignity and respect:

After quitting an abusive relationship, you need to remind yourself that you deserve to be respected, loved and cared for the right way. Having a closed heart and being guarded comes naturally after being in an abusive relationship. But you need to allow the right people to help you out as well. You can join a self-help group or community where you can confide freely and get the necessary help and support.

7. Practice self-love:

Start to know, understand and love yourself first. Put yourself and your needs as a top priority in your life, however difficult it might be to put into practice.

Once you know to do the same, you will learn to differentiate between healthy and toxic attachments. It is a good time to practice the things that you once loved but are no longer practicing, speak to old pals who you lost touch with, and take yourself out on a date if needs to be. Remind yourself each day that you are strong and there will be a better future tomorrow.

8. Forgive:

It is important for you to realise that narcissism is a mental illness. In many of the cases, the narcissist was dealing with their own internal turmoil and chaos, which they have not come to terms with and refuse to do so. It is as difficult as it sounds; practice forgiveness. The anger, vengeance, guilt, and the overall dead weight, you hold on to, will only hamper your healing journey ahead.

9. Disengagement:

In cases of shared parenting, it is advisable to remain disengaged and not talk about personal matters that would trigger any kind of reaction. Talk about things that are neutral both in front of the kids and even otherwise. For example, 'Hey, did you guys have a nice weekend?'

This helps and reminds the narcissist that you do not want to feed into their ego-validating games anymore. This way, you also remind yourself that you can let go and move on with your life.

10. Don't rush into a new relationship:

Although it is a personal choice, you need to remember you chose to separate yourself to prioritise and restore self-preservation. You had lost a part of yourself and your identity to the narcissist. It is important to find yourself first. Even if you are getting close to someone, give yourself time to heal and do not make the other person the *sole* source of your healing.

11. Be supportive to others in similar situation:

You have no idea how much your kind words of support and encouragement would mean to someone who needs to hear them. Having gone through a similar phase yourself and on the healing journey, you can very well uplift someone who needs help, making your healing journey more fruitful and gratifying.

The process of healing will be different for every survivor, depending upon the tenure and extent of abuse suffered by them while in a narcissistic bond. Hence, even if you progress slowly or see yourself going back and forth, questioning your decisions, remind yourself that this is normal and you will make it through this phase.

B. The next important step here is to make up the right mindset after detachment:

In order to start the healing process, you need to remind yourself that:

- You have a distinct self who is confident and capable of deciding for yourself.
- You are identifying the trends that have held you back from becoming yourself and stop appeasing behaviour patterns that no longer serve your higher good.

Once you are well-positioned mentally (the time frame for which will differ for every survivor), you will be able to identify better and healthier alternatives to managing your emotions.

C. Developing and nurturing self-respect:

A narcissist will in all possible ways show you that they do not respect you. You don't have any value other than your immediate utility to help them meet their goals. If you have been exposed to this pattern of disregard and disrespect for too long, you start losing your own sense of self-worth.

After separation from a narcissist, it is of prime importance to reclaim the sense of respect, first within you and then to the outside world. You need to reiterate to yourself constantly:

- You choose to be your own distinct self.
- You will now only focus on building yourself up to your full potential.
- You will be only driven by love, most importantly; love for yourself.
- You choose to be free; free to make your own choices and would be happy for others to make their own choices, too.
- You are motivated by encouragement. Now, you only seek people who encourage you and others.
- You choose to be open and appreciate honesty and transparency.
- You embrace yourself in totality, both your strengths and weaknesses.
- You only treat others the way you would wish to be treated.
- You understand that holding grudges drains you, and you choose to forgive and move on so as to get the right people in.
- You do not claim to be a perfectionist but a "work in progress' till the last day of your life.

In the path of healing, it is important to reclaim self-respect first, as it is not something that anyone can give you. It was always there in you but was badly bruised and taken for granted while you were subjected to narcissistic abuse. Initially, it will be very difficult to think differently on the above-mentioned points.

Doubting your own self-worth immediately after separation is quite common. Moving ahead, self-respect and self-worth are two things you cannot let anyone fool around with anymore. They should be the bedrock and foundation of your healing process.

D. Inner child healing:

We have all heard of this phrase quite often but find it difficult to pursue supporting activities on a daily basis. There is a grown-up version of us who can go to work, pay the bills, take care of the family, etc., but we often forget to heal and nurture the child in us. If, unfortunately, we were abused or traumatized as a child, it is of great importance to heal our inner child to be content and optimistic in life.

More often than not, survivors of narcissistic abuse suffer without being aware that they were in a toxic bond. This happens a lot because of their childhood trauma, as explained in Chapter II.

So, besides the above-mentioned points on how our 'adult self' needs to heal, let us look at a few basic activities that we all, and in this context, a survivor of an abusive relationship can do very easily:

1. Write letters:

Write letters to reflect on the feelings you had in the past and the feelings that you continue to carry now. You can write letters to your parents (living or deceased), the parents you always wished you had, to your past self, or to the person you wish to be.

These letters are not meant to be posted (if you choose to write to someone in person). They could find their place in your dairy or a journal. The purpose behind writing letters is to allow ourselves to express the feelings that we haven't had the opportunity to share for a long time, and definitely not as children.

Do not hold back from penning down your regrets and grudges in the journey of growing up as a child, an adolescent and as an adult. Also do not forget to write about your accomplishments and how far you have made it in your healing journey.

Writing letters will not only make your emotions flow but also remind you of incidents that you wish never happened. Look at it like a self-counselling session, where you are pouring your heart and mind out to no one but yourself, reflecting on your past, present, and future, and trying to address your innermost feelings.

However tough it may seem, your feelings (especially the ones unrecognized and disregarded) need to be addressed. Refrain from judging yourself harshly and calling out names, like 'lazy', 'foolish', etc.

Choose a convenient time in the day and do whatever makes it comfortable for you to write... like adjusting the lighting in the house, putting on your favourite music... etc. You will realise while writing, as to how many unsaid and pent-up emotions you have inside you that needed to come out.

2. Have a dialogue with yourself sometimes:

The way we talk to ourselves is the way we talk to our inner child. Most of us speak in a way the grownups had spoken to us while we were a child. We internalize them and unknowingly keep practicing behaviour patterns that hurt us and do not facilitate our inner child healing.

So, engage in positive and compassionate dialogues with yourself. Replace competitive or compulsive phrases, like 'had to', 'supposed to', 'need to', etc., with more positive words, like 'I would like to', 'I get to', 'it would feel good to', etc. For example:

> ➤ It would actually be helpful to set some healthy boundaries or
> ➤ I would want to get more sleep or eat right to feel fit.

Positive dialogue is necessary on a daily basis to identify and eliminate negative thoughts and behaviour patterns that we unconsciously carry in our minds.

3. Engage in art and play:

If you had a difficult or strict childhood where not much was done to facilitate your creative side, engage in those undone or unfinished activities now. Join a dance class, paint or simply create stuff with the play dough. Even if you were encouraged and did pursue certain activities as a child, start practicing them now. Merely a trip to your favourite beach to play with the sand and soak your feet in the water can uplift your spirits throughout the day!

4. Rest:

Resting is inner child work, and unfortunately, many of us do not understand this. By getting enough sleep or by being rested, we are telling both our inner child and grown-up self that our needs are important.

Just as important as work and family are, so is our own mental and physical health. Lack of rest reflects on our work and overall life. Hence, resting is a big part of your healing process.

The above-mentioned points will also help if you are going through a counselling or therapy session. You can do one or all of them on a daily basis as an additional activity for your healing process.

E. Healing from Narcissistic Parental wounds:

If you are someone who has faced narcissistic abuse at the hands of a parent(s), here are certain pointers that you should work on:

1. Forgiveness:

Forgiving a parent is especially challenging; they are not only related to us by bloodline but also the first people in this world whom we learn to trust by default. However, forgiving as a process is especially important if you are trying to rebuild or reconcile your differences with your parent(s).

We need to acknowledge that our parents are humans, hence flawed and have hurt us in ways that we did not expect. Make a comparative table listing incidents connected to them that hurt you as a child or even as a grown-up and those incidents that really brought you joy.

There should have been instances where they supported you, stood up for you, or just showed up when you needed them. This comparison will enable you to realise that they tried doing their best as parents and, in the process, went wrong quite a few times, which hurt you.

You will understand this even better if you are a parent yourself. Not to justify your parents' actions, but you know there could have been instances where you were not your best as a parent, too. If you can relate to them and forgive yourself, you certainly can extend the same courtesy towards our parents.

Know that their actions and shortcomings are not a reflection of your worth:

It is important to remind yourselves that the way your parents could not show up for you or disappointed you, is not a reflection of who you have become.

Not many of us know how our parents grew up or were treated as children. Some parents do narrate their dreaded childhood memories to their children, but that is only to remind themselves and their children that they are much better parents. Not justifying their actions towards us once again, but you need to understand that 'no one can pour from an empty cup'.

Parents cannot show those emotions or feelings that they have been deprived of as children. They, perhaps, were never able to let go of their grudges towards their parents, did slightly better than them as parents, and constantly reminded you of how they were better parents and how lucky you were to have them as parents.

It is not that they couldn't have chosen a better path, but they chose to stick around the same negative behaviour patterns and, in the process, hurt you in unexpected ways. The question is, do you as a parent now, need to repeat the same cycle again?

Toxic parents, sadly, fail to understand that being a parent is a matter of **choice** and a **privilege** that the universe grants us. They see a part of them growing up in this world. Their behaviour, words and actions shape how their children perceive their world to be.

2. Accept the healing and quit the past karma:

This is important, especially if you are a parent yourself. Your children will grow up in a safe and healthy hologram only if you first accept your own healing process.

Unfortunately, if you had parents who could not be there for you, you need to come out of that karmic pattern and stop repeating those same mistakes. You need to take a leap of faith and come out of the perceptions and expectations your family had about you.

This step is difficult, especially if you were judged, ridiculed, bullied or called names as you were growing up. You cannot be your authentic self, attract the right people in your life and be the person you want to be as an adult. You fumble and juggle good people and end up in the wrong relationships, causing a greater imbalance in your life.

Healthy families celebrate each other and support one another. Toxic families are the exact opposite of this, and if, unfortunately, you have a toxic family, you might have wrong notions and unhealthy behaviour patterns that reflect on your work and relationships. If you allow your past to control you, it will soon start to show in the way your children feel about themselves and treat others.

It is, therefore, very important to break free from the past by forgiving those who wronged you and focusing on your own healing. Seek professional counselling or self-help groups to help you in the process. You will realise that you are not alone and that there are many who went through a bad childhood but still trying to be ideal parents to their kids.

3. Re-parenting:

The process of re-parenting needs the inner child healing. All the points mentioned above in the 'inner child healing' process will come handy once you are able to forgive your parents. Do not disregard any negative emotions; communicate openly to yourself, acknowledge, and then learn to let go and improvise. Practice self-love and self-care and maintain healthy boundaries with people who do not serve your highest good.

Conclusion:

Coming out of narcissistic abuse, whether parental or with a partner, is never easy. The healing process is different for each survivor. It is imperative to remind ourselves that we are not alone in this healing journey, regain self-respect and get proper help and support to find and focus on our strengths.

www.ingramcontent.com/pod-product-compliance
Lightning Source LLC
LaVergne TN
LVHW061623070526
838199LV00078B/7400